NECESSARY
PAPERWORK

ISBN: 978-1518824968

Gerst, Ellen
Necessary Paperwork: A Guide to the Details of Your Life

NECESSARY PAPERWORK

A guide for your family on

the details of your life

Ellen Gerst

TABLE OF CONTENTS

INTRODUCTION

The death or, before that event occurs, the diminishing mental capacity of a close loved one for which you are caring brings untold grief, as well as a never-ending stream of confusion and paperwork.

If you have spent many weeks looking for important paperwork, phone numbers of people who you need to contact, prior medical records, or have been generally frustrated by messy recordkeeping, you have the ability to save your own family from this same disastrous scenario.

By filling in the forms contained in this book, you can have a guide for your caregivers and/or heirs to follow. It steers you through the many aspects of your life and the things you need to relay to your loved ones.

When you have completed this task, take the entire book to a bank or another place where you can have your signature notarized. That act will make this book a legal and enforceable document.

After signing it, if there are changes to be made, simply add in the information on the Addendum Pages at the end of the book and reference the original section. Date and sign each Addendum and also have it notarized.

You've taken an important step in this process by purchasing this book. Why not start this project today? If you're hesitating, remember the wise words of Janet Dailey, who said the following.

"Someday in NOT a day of the week!"

FOOD FOR THOUGHT

In the introduction, I've outlined a straightforward path to help you to get your affairs in order. This is not just a task to complete as you enter your "golden years" but rather one to embark upon early and continually update as your life changes.

Although you probably know that you "should" do this, procrastination often gets the better of most people. However, you may want to think about procrastination as Christopher Parker describes it as follows.

> *"Procrastination is like a credit card.*
> *It's a lot of fun until you get the bill."*

As a former young widow, I know the unexpected happens and that you can be left with a mess. Not only can sickness come on suddenly, accidents happen. Furthermore, as a caregiver of a mother with Alzheimer's, I know that the *golden years* can quickly change to the *wonder years* when memory starts to fail and a person starts to *wonder* where important documents, jewelry, etc. are squirreled away in places thought to be safe.

I know it's easy to put off this important task, but as Benjamin Franklin said, *"You may delay, but time will not."* Moreover, *if* the unexpected happens, you will wish that you had started on this endeavor today.

Although it may be necessary for you to devote a fair amount of time to this project, once you start, it will begin to flow. You'll find yourself on a roll as you gather the pertinent information and be filled with a sense of purpose and accomplishment when the task is complete.

> *"It is easier to resist at the beginning than at the end."*
>
> ~Leonardo da Vinci~

THOUGHTS ON ORGANIZING YOUR LIFE

Filling out this book is an exercise in organization. When it's completed, and you look at it in totality, you may realize you have too much "stuff" or your life is overly complicated. If so, here are some thoughts to consider.

*Organizing is something you do BEFORE you do
something so that when you do it, it is not all mixed up.*
~A.A. Milne~

*Being organized isn't about getting rid of everything you own
or trying to become a different person.
It's about living the way you want to live, but better.*
~Andrew Mellon~

Everything you "have to have" owns you.
~Wayne Dyer~

Everything you release gives you freedom.
~Maggie Reyes~

Organize, don't agonize.
~Nancy Pelosi~

Four Tenets of Organization

1. Be organized. You don't have to be perfect.

2. Less stuff equals more time to enjoy the stuff you already own.

3. Control your clutter or it will take over your life and control you.

4. Organized people are simply lazy ones who don't want to spend time looking for things.

FORMS

IMPORTANT PEOPLE

IMPORTANT PEOPLE

IMMEDIATE FAMILY

Name _____

Relationship _____

Address _____

E-mail _____

Phone # _____

Name _____

Relationship _____

Address _____

E-mail _____

Phone # _____

Name _____

Relationship _____

Address _____

E-mail _____

Phone # _____

Name _____

Relationship _____

Address _____

E-mail _____

Phone # _____

Name _____

Relationship _____

Address _____

E-mail _____

Phone # _____

IMMEDIATE FAMILY

Name _____

Relationship _____

Address _____

E-mail _____

Phone # _____

Name _____

Relationship _____

Address _____

E-mail _____

Phone # _____

Name _____

Relationship _____

Address _____

E-mail _____

Phone # _____

Name _____

Relationship _____

Address _____

E-mail _____

Phone # _____

Name _____

Relationship _____

Address _____

E-mail _____

Phone # _____

CLOSE FRIENDS AND OTHER RELATIVES

Name _____

Relationship _____

Address _____

E-mail _____

Phone # _____

Name _____

Relationship _____

Address _____

E-mail _____

Phone # _____

Name _____

Relationship _____

Address _____

E-mail _____

Phone # _____

Name _____

Relationship _____

Address _____

E-mail _____

Phone # _____

Name _____

Relationship _____

Address _____

E-mail _____

Phone # _____

CLOSE FRIENDS AND OTHER RELATIVES

Name _____

Relationship _____

Address _____

E-mail _____

Phone # _____

Name _____

Relationship _____

Address _____

E-mail _____

Phone # _____

Name _____

Relationship _____

Address _____

E-mail _____

Phone # _____

PETS

Name(s)/Nickname(s) _____

Age(s) _____ Breed(s) _____

Normal Weight _____ Brand of Food _____

Type of Snacks/How Often? _____

Veterinarian _____

Address/Phone # _____

Last Check-up _____

Rabies/Other Vaccines _____

Exercise Regimen _____

Favorite Kennel Info _____

_____

Others To Be Notified In Case of Illness/Accident/Death

Name _____

Relationship _____

Address _____

E-mail _____

Phone # _____

Name _____

Relationship _____

Address _____

E-mail _____

Phone # _____

Name _____

Relationship _____

Address _____

E-mail _____

Phone # _____

Name _____

Relationship _____

Address _____

E-mail _____

Phone # _____

Name _____

Relationship _____

Address _____

E-mail _____

Phone # _____

GUARDIANS OF UNDERAGE CHILDREN AND THOSE WHO CAN WATCH CHILDREN IN AN EMERGENCY SITUATION

Name _____

Relationship _____

Address _____

E-mail _____

Phone # _____

Name _____

Relationship _____

Address _____

E-mail _____

Phone # _____

Name _____

Relationship _____

Address _____

E-mail _____

Phone # _____

Name _____

Relationship _____

Address _____

E-mail _____

Phone # _____

Name _____

Relationship _____

Address _____

E-mail _____

Phone # _____

OTHERS THAT CAN HELP IN A GENERAL EMERGENCY

Name   _____

Relationship   _____

Address   _____

E-mail   _____

Phone #   _____

Name   _____

Relationship   _____

Address   _____

E-mail   _____

Phone #   _____

Name   _____

Relationship   _____

Address   _____

E-mail   _____

Phone #   _____

Name   _____

Relationship   _____

Address   _____

E-mail   _____

Phone #   _____

Name   _____

Relationship   _____

Address   _____

E-mail   _____

Phone #   _____

EXECUTOR OF ESTATE

Name _____

Relationship _____

Address _____

E-mail _____

Phone # _____

Name _____

Relationship _____

Address _____

E-mail _____

Phone # _____

PERSONAL REPRESENTATIVE(S)

Name _____

Relationship _____

Address _____

E-mail _____

Phone # _____

Name _____

Relationship _____

Address _____

E-mail _____

Phone # _____

NOTES

_____

_____

_____

_____

ATTORNEY/LAW FIRM

Name _____

Type/Firm _____

Address _____

E-mail _____

Phone # _____

Name _____

Type/Firm _____

Address _____

E-mail _____

Phone # _____

Name _____

Type/Firm _____

Address _____

E-mail _____

Phone # _____

Name _____

Type/Firm _____

Address _____

E-mail _____

Phone # _____

Name _____

Type/Firm _____

Address _____

E-mail _____

Phone # _____

ACCOUNTANT/CPA FIRM

Name _____

Relationship _____

Address _____

E-mail _____

Phone # _____

Name _____

Relationship _____

Address _____

E-mail _____

Phone # _____

FINANCIAL PLANNER

Name _____

Relationship _____

Address _____

E-mail _____

Phone # _____

Name _____

Relationship _____

Address _____

E-mail _____

Phone # _____

NOTES

_____

_____

_____

_____

MEDICAL: PHYSICIANS

Name _____

Specialty _____

Address _____

E-mail _____

Phone # _____

Name _____

Specialty _____

Address _____

E-mail _____

Phone # _____

Name _____

Specialty _____

Address _____

E-mail _____

Phone # _____

Name _____

Specialty _____

Address _____

E-mail _____

Phone # _____

Name _____

Specialty _____

Address _____

E-mail _____

Phone # _____

MEDICAL: PHYSICIANS

Name   _____

Specialty   _____

Address   _____

E-mail   _____

Phone #   _____

Name   _____

Specialty   _____

Address   _____

E-mail   _____

Phone #   _____

Name   _____

Specialty   _____

Address   _____

E-mail   _____

Phone #   _____

Name   _____

Specialty   _____

Address   _____

E-mail   _____

Phone #   _____

Name   _____

Specialty   _____

Address   _____

E-mail   _____

Phone #   _____

MEDICAL: DENTIST: GENERAL, ORTHO, PERIO, ORAL SURGEON

Name   _____

Specialty   _____

Address   _____

E-mail   _____

Phone #   _____

Name   _____

Specialty   _____

Address   _____

E-mail   _____

Phone #   _____

Name   _____

Specialty   _____

Address   _____

E-mail   _____

Phone #   _____

Name   _____

Specialty   _____

Address   _____

E-mail   _____

Phone #   _____

Name   _____

Specialty   _____

Address   _____

E-mail   _____

Phone #   _____

PREFERRED HOSPITAL #1

Name   _____

Address   _____

_____

Phone #   _____

PREFERRED HOSPITAL #2

Name   _____

Address   _____

_____

Phone #   _____

PREFERRED PHARMACY #1

Name   _____

Address   _____

_____

Phone #   _____

PREFERRED PHARMACY #2

Name   _____

Address   _____

_____

Phone #   _____

NOTES

_____

_____

_____

_____

BUSINESS PARTNERS

Name _____

Business _____

Address _____

E-mail _____

Phone # _____

Name _____

Business _____

Address _____

E-mail _____

Phone # _____

Name _____

Business _____

Address _____

E-mail _____

Phone # _____

Name _____

Business _____

Address _____

E-mail _____

Phone # _____

NOTES

_____

_____

_____

_____

_____

_____

INSURANCE AGENTS FOR VARIOUS POLICIES *(Detail about policies in next section)*

INSURANCE AGENT/BROKER #1: PERSONAL

Name _____

Address _____

_____

Phone # _____

INSURANCE AGENT/BROKER #2: THROUGH WORK

Name _____

Address _____

_____

Phone # _____

INSURANCE AGENT/BROKER #3: THROUGH VETERAN'S AFFAIRS

Name _____

Address _____

_____

Phone # _____

INSURANCE AGENT/BROKER #4: OTHER

Name _____

Address _____

_____

Phone # _____

NOTES

_____

_____

IMPORTANT DOCUMENTS AND THEIR LOCATIONS

IMPORTANT DOCUMENTS AND THEIR LOCATION

WILL

Location   _____

Attorney   _____

Address   _____

E-mail   _____

Phone #   _____

TRUST DOCUMENTS

Location   _____

Grantor (person who set up trust)   _____

Irrevocable or Revocable?_____

Attorney   _____

Address   _____

E-mail   _____

Phone #   _____

Trustee   _____

Relationship   _____

Address   _____

E-mail   _____

Phone #   _____

TRUST DOCUMENTS

Location   _____

Grantor (person who set up trust)   _____

Irrevocable or Revocable?_____

Attorney   _____

Address   _____

E-mail   _____

Phone #   _____

TRUST DOCUMENTS *(continued)*

Trustee _____

Relationship _____

Address _____

E-mail _____

Phone # _____

BUSINESS AGREEMENTS/SELF-EMPLOYED COMPANY DOCUMENTS

Location of Business _____

Name of Company _____

Partner _____

Phone # _____

Address _____

E-mail _____

Website and Login Information _____

_____

Other Important Employees To Contact _____

_____

_____

Stock Certificates? _____

Location of Books and Records _____

_____

If Records Are Online, Password _____

Business Agreements/Partnership Papers _____

Who takes over in case of death or illness? _____

_____

Other Pertinent Information _____

_____

_____

_____

_____

VEHICLE TITLES: VEHICLE #1

Vehicle Description _____

VIN # _____

Vehicle Housed _____

Lien Holder(s) _____

Address _____

Phone # _____   E-mail _____

Amount Owing _____   Monthly Payment Due Date _____

VEHICLE TITLES: VEHICLE #2

Vehicle Description _____

VIN # _____

Vehicle Housed _____

Lien Holder(s) _____

Address _____

Phone # _____   E-mail _____

Amount Owing _____   Monthly Payment Due Date _____

VEHICLE TITLES: VEHICLE #3

Vehicle Description _____

VIN # _____

Vehicle Housed _____

Lien Holder(s) _____

Address _____

Phone # _____   E-mail _____

Amount Owing _____   Monthly Payment Due Date _____

SAFE DEPOSIT BOX

Housed at _____

Location _____

Phone # _____

Key Location _____

Who Has Access _____

LOCATION OF INSURANCE POLICIES *(details in another section)*

Life _____

Health _____

Auto _____

Disability _____

Homeowner's _____

Rental Property _____

Long Term Care _____

MORTGAGE

Property Address _____

Lien Holder _____

Address _____

Phone #/Email _____

Homeowner's _____

Rental Property _____

OTHER DOCUMENTS

Marriage Certificate _____

Divorce Decree _____

Birth Certificate _____

Tax Returns _____

Funeral/Cemetery Arrangements _____

Passport _____

Medical Records _____

DETAILED

INSURANCE

POLICY

INFORMATION

DETAILED INSURANCE INFORMATION

INSURANCE

Not all the information requested below will apply to each person or policy. To help you fill out these forms, information to be gathered includes the following:

1. Is there more than one policy? Are the life insurance policies term or whole life? Where is the paperwork located?

2. Is the policy owned by the individual, a revocable trust, an irrevocable trust?

3. If the individual is ill, you don't want any policies to lapse because of non or late payment. Determine the premium due date.

4. Were any loans taken out against any of the policies that would reduce benefits?

5. Are the beneficiaries clearly named and all property titled properly?

6. Was the policy written through work, Veteran's Administration, other?

LIFE INSURANCE: POLICY #1

Policy # _____

Agent _____

Phone # _____

E-mail _____

Type of Coverage _____

Owner of Policy _____

Current Death Benefit Amount _____

Current Cash Value _____

Premium Amount _____

LIFE INSURANCE POLICY #1 *(continued)*

Payment Due Date _____

Amount of Current Loans Against Policy _____

Beneficiaries _____

_____

_____

_____

LIFE INSURANCE: POLICY #2

Policy # _____

Agent _____

Phone # _____

E-mail _____

Type of Coverage _____

Owner of Policy _____

Current Death Benefit Amount _____

Current Cash Value _____

Premium Amount _____

Payment Due Date _____

Amount of Current Loans Against Policy _____

Beneficiaries _____

_____

_____

_____

NOTES/MORE INFO

_____

_____

_____

_____

LIFE INSURANCE: POLICY #3

Policy # _____

Agent _____

Phone # _____

E-mail _____

Type of Coverage _____

Owner of Policy _____

Current Death Benefit Amount _____

Current Cash Value _____

Premium Amount _____

Payment Due Date _____

Amount of Current Loans Against Policy _____

Beneficiaries _____

_____

_____

_____

LIFE INSURANCE: POLICY #4

Policy # _____

Agent _____

Phone # _____

E-mail _____

Type of Coverage _____

Owner of Policy _____

Current Death Benefit Amount _____

Current Cash Value _____

Premium Amount _____

Payment Due Date _____

Amount of Current Loans Against Policy _____

Beneficiaries _____

_____

HEALTH INSURANCE POLICY #1 (PRIVATE)

Policy # _____

Agent _____

Phone # _____

E-mail _____

Deductible _____

Ratio of Coverage_____

Premium _____ Due Date_____

Is Certification Necessary Before a Procedure? _____

Pharmacy Coverage?_____

HEALTH INSURANCE POLICY #2 (THROUGH WORK)

Policy # _____

Agent _____

Phone # _____

E-mail _____

Deductible _____

Ratio of Coverage_____

Premium _____ Due Date_____

Is Certification Necessary Before a Procedure? _____

Pharmacy Coverage? _____

HEALTH INSURANCE POLICY #3 (SUPPLEMENTAL)

Policy # _____

Agent _____

Phone # _____

E-mail _____

Deductible _____

Ratio of Coverage_____

Premium _____ Due Date_____

Is Certification Necessary Before a Procedure? _____

Pharmacy Coverage?_____

HEALTH INSURANCE POLICY #4 (LONG TERM CARE)

Policy # _____

Agent _____

Phone # _____

E-mail _____

Deductible _____

Ratio of Coverage_____

Premium _____ Due Date _____

Is Certification Necessary Before Hiring Care? _____

Are Only Certain Classes of Caregivers Covered, i.e. CNA or LPN? _____

HEALTH INSURANCE POLICY #5 (WORKMAN'S COMP BENEFITS)

Policy # _____

Contact _____

Phone # _____

E-mail _____

Deductible _____

Date of Disability _____

Length of Coverage _____

Coverage Beginning Date _____ Ending Date _____

Pharmacy Coverage?_____

HEALTH INSURANCE #6 (DISABILITY)

Policy # _____

Contact _____

Phone # _____

E-mail _____

Deductible _____

Date of Disability _____

Length of Coverage _____

Coverage Beginning Date _____ Ending Date _____

Pharmacy Coverage? _____

HOMEOWNER'S POLICY

Property Address _____

Policy # _____

Agent _____

Phone # _____

E-mail _____

Coverage _____

Premium _____ Due Date_____

Notes _____

HOMEOWNER'S POLICY (RENTAL PROPERTY)

Property Address _____

Policy # _____

Agent _____

Phone # _____

E-mail _____

Coverage _____

Premium _____ Due Date_____

Notes _____

UMBRELLA POLICY

Property Address _____

Policy # _____

Agent _____

Phone # _____

E-mail _____

Coverage _____

Premium _____ Due Date_____

Notes _____

VEHICLE POLICY

Policy # _____

Agent _____

Phone # _____

E-mail _____

Vehicle/VIN _____

Premium _____   Due Date_____

Liability Deductible _____

Uninsured/Underinsured Coverage?_____

BOAT/RECREATIONAL/MOTORCYCLE POLICY

Policy # _____

Agent _____

Phone # _____

E-mail _____

Vehicle/VIN _____

Premium _____   Due Date_____

Liability Deductible _____

Uninsured/Underinsured Coverage? _____

OTHER VEHICLE POLICY

Policy # _____

Agent _____

Phone # _____

E-mail _____

Vehicle/VIN _____

Premium _____   Due Date_____

Liability Deductible _____

Uninsured/Underinsured Coverage?_____

ADDITIONAL POLICY

Type _____

Policy # _____

Agent _____

Phone # _____

E-mail _____

Deductible _____

Coverage _____

Premium _____ Due Date_____

ADDITIONAL POLICY

Type _____

Policy # _____

Agent _____

Phone # _____

E-mail _____

Deductible _____

Coverage _____

Premium _____ Due Date_____

MISCELLANEOUS NOTES ON POLICIES

Copies of Policies Can Be Found in These Locations:

☐ Desk Drawer _____

☐ Filing Cabinet _____

☐ Safe Deposit Box _____

☐ Other _____

☐ Other _____

☐ Other _____

☐ Other _____

HOUSEHOLD INFORMATION

OVERVIEW: DETAILS ABOUT MY HOME

I live in _____ (city, state) in an _____
(apartment, single family home, mobile home, other).

My rent/mortgage payment is _____, and I have a
homeowner's association monthly charge of _____. The utility
companies providing service to my home include:
_____ (electric); _____ (gas);
_____ (water); _____
(security/house alarm); _____ (cable
TV); _____ (Internet services); _____
(sanitation/sewer); _____ (landline telephone); and
_____ (mobile telephone).

My electric usage is on a Time Demand basis, which means that it's
more expensive for me to use appliances and run air
conditioning/heat during these hours: _____.
I only run my dishwasher, washing machine and dryer on the
following days/during the following hours: _____
_____.
During the summer, I keep my home at _____degrees during the day
and _____degrees overnight. During the colder months, I keep my
home at ____ degrees during the day and ____ degrees overnight.

Trash pick up occurs on the following days: _____
(regular) and _____ (recycle).

The sprinkler system for the lawn and plants follows this schedule:
_____
_____.

The pool is cleaned on these days, including back washing:
_____.

The lawn is mowed by (myself/landscaper) on these days:
_____.

HOUSEHOLD ACCOUNTS

MORTGAGE

Holder of Note _____

Balance   _____

Address   _____

Phone #   _____

E-mail   _____

Payment Amount _____

Due Date   _____ Late After Date _____

RENT

Rental Agent   _____

Monthly Rent _____

Address   _____

Phone #   _____

E-mail   _____

Due Date   _____ Late After Date _____

Lease Terms   _____

HOMEOWNER'S ASSOCIATION FEE

HOA Name   _____

Address   _____

Phone #   _____

Contact Name _____ E-mail _____

Payment Amount _____ per year/quarter/month

UTILITIES

ELECTRIC

Company Name   _____

Account #   _____

Phone #   _____

GAS

Company Name _____

Account # _____

Phone # _____

WATER

Company Name _____

Account # _____

Phone # _____

INTERNET PROVIDER

Company Name _____

Account # _____

Phone # _____

CABLE/SATELLITE TV PROVIDER

Company Name _____

Account # _____

Phone # _____

LAND LINE TELEPHONE PROVIDER

Company Name _____

Account # _____

Phone # _____

CELL PHONE PROVIDER

Company Name _____

Account # _____

Phone # _____

SEWER/SANITATION PROVIDER

Company Name _____

Account # _____

Phone # _____

OTHER MONTHLY EXPENSES

GYM MEMBERSHIP

Gym Name _____

Account # _____ Monthly Dues_____

Address _____

Phone # _____

SECURITY/ALARM PROVIDER

Company Name _____

Account # _____ Monthly Amount_____

Phone # _____

LANDSCAPE PROVIDER

Company Name _____

Account # _____ Monthly Amount_____

Phone # _____

POOL SERVICE PROVIDER

Company Name _____

Account # _____ Monthly Amount_____

Phone # _____

HOME CLEANING PROVIDER

Company Name _____

Account # _____ Monthly Amount _____

Phone # _____

OTHER PROVIDER

Company Name _____

Account # _____

Phone # _____

OTHER PROVIDER

Company Name _____

Account # _____

Phone # _____

PERSONAL ASSETS

PERSONAL ASSETS

CASH AND CASH EQUIVALENTS
BANK ACCOUNTS/BROKERAGE ACCOUNTS/CDS

Name of Institution _____ Account # _____

Address _____

Contact _____ Telephone # _____

Type of Account _____ Average Balance _____

Name of Institution _____ Account # _____

Address _____

Contact _____ Telephone # _____

Type of Account _____ Average Balance _____

Name of Institution _____ Account # _____

Address _____

Contact _____ Telephone # _____

Type of Account _____ Average Balance _____

Name of Institution _____ Account # _____

Address _____

Contact _____ Telephone # _____

Type of Account _____ Average Balance _____

Name of Institution _____ Account # _____

Address _____

Contact _____ Telephone # _____

Type of Account _____ Average Balance _____

Name of Institution _____ Account # _____

Address _____

Contact _____ Telephone # _____

Type of Account _____ Average Balance _____

Name of Institution _____ Account # _____

Address _____

Contact _____ Telephone # _____

Type of Account _____ Average Balance _____

Name of Institution _____ Account # _____

Address _____

Contact _____ Telephone # _____

Type of Account _____ Average Balance _____

Name of Institution _____ Account # _____

Address _____

Contact _____ Telephone # _____

Type of Account _____ Average Balance _____

Name of Institution _____ Account # _____

Address _____

Contact _____ Telephone # _____

Type of Account _____ Average Balance _____

Name of Institution _____ Account # _____

Address _____

Contact _____ Telephone # _____

Type of Account _____ Average Balance _____

Name of Institution _____ Account # _____

Address _____

Contact _____ Telephone # _____

Type of Account _____ Average Balance _____

Name of Institution _____ Account # _____

Address _____

Contact _____ Telephone # _____

Type of Account _____ Average Balance _____

INVESTMENTS
MUTUAL FUNDS/T-BILLS/BONDS/BUSINESSES

Type of Investment _____ Account # _____

Investment Company _____

Address _____

Contact _____ Telephone # _____

Approximate Current Value _____ as of __/__/__

Type of Investment _____ Account # _____

Investment Company _____

Address _____

Contact _____ Telephone # _____

Approximate Current Value _____ as of __/__/__

Type of Investment _____ Account # _____

Investment Company _____

Address _____

Contact _____ Telephone # _____

Approximate Current Value _____ as of __/__/__

Type of Investment _____ Account # _____

Investment Company _____

Address _____

Contact _____ Telephone # _____

Approximate Current Value _____ as of __/__/__

Type of Investment _____ Account # _____

Investment Company _____

Address _____

Contact _____ Telephone # _____

Approximate Current Value _____ as of __/__/__

Type of Investment _____ Account # _____

Investment Company _____

Address _____

Contact _____ Telephone # _____

Approximate Current Value _____ as of __/__/__

Type of Investment _____ Account # _____

Investment Company _____

Address _____

Contact _____ Telephone # _____

Approximate Current Value _____ as of __/__/__

Type of Investment _____ Account # _____

Investment Company _____

Address _____

Contact _____ Telephone # _____

Approximate Current Value _____ as of __/__/__

Type of Investment _____ Account # _____

Investment Company _____

Address _____

Contact _____ Telephone # _____

Approximate Current Value _____ as of __/__/__

Type of Investment _____ Account # _____

Investment Company _____

Address _____

Contact _____ Telephone # _____

Approximate Current Value _____ as of __/__/__

Type of Investment _____ Account # _____

Investment Company _____

Address _____

Contact _____ Telephone # _____

Approximate Current Value _____ as of __/__/__

RETIREMENT PLANS

Type of Plan: IRA, KEOGH, 401K, DBPP, Annuity, Other (circle one)

Broker/Trustee _____

Address _____

Account # _____ Telephone # _____

Location of Paperwork _____

Approximate Value _____ as of __/__/__

Beneficiary/Contact Information_____

_____

Type of Plan: IRA, KEOGH, 401K, DBPP, Annuity, Other (circle one)

Broker/Trustee _____

Address _____

Account # _____ Telephone # _____

Location of Paperwork _____

Approximate Value _____ as of __/__/__

Beneficiary/Contact Information_____

_____

Type of Plan: IRA, KEOGH, 401K, DBPP, Annuity, Other (circle one)

Broker/Trustee _____

Address _____

Account # _____ Telephone # _____

Location of Paperwork _____

Approximate Value _____ as of __/__/__

Beneficiary/Contact Information_____

_____

Type of Plan: IRA, KEOGH, 401K, DBPP, Annuity, Other (circle one)

Broker/Trustee _____

Address _____

Account # _____ Telephone # _____

Location of Paperwork _____

Approximate Value _____ as of __/__/__

Beneficiary/Contact Information_____

_____

Type of Plan: IRA, KEOGH, 401K, DBPP, Annuity, Other (circle one)

Broker/Trustee _____

Address _____

Account # _____ Telephone # _____

Location of Paperwork _____

Approximate Value _____ as of __/__/__

Beneficiary/Contact Information_____

_____

RENTAL PROPERTY GENERATING INCOME

Address #1_____

Rental Price _____ Length of Lease _____

Use Airbnb? _____ Account # _____

Utility Providers _____

_____

Mortgage Info _____

Caretaker Name/# _____

Insurance Information _____

_____

Address #2 _____

Rental Price _____ Length of Lease _____

Use Airbnb? _____ Account # _____

Utility Providers _____

_____

Mortgage Info _____

Caretaker Name/# _____

Insurance Information _____

NOTES RECEIVABLE

Description _____

Face Value _____ From Whom _____

Address of Payor _____

Telephone # of Payor _____

Location of Paperwork _____

Collateral _____

Note Terms/Interest Rate _____ Due Date _____

_____

_____

Description _____

Face Value _____ From Whom _____

Address of Payor _____

Telephone # of Payor _____

Location of Paperwork _____

Collateral _____

Note Terms/Interest Rate _____ Due Date _____

_____

_____

Description _____

Face Value _____ From Whom _____

Address of Payor _____

Telephone # of Payor _____

Location of Paperwork _____

Collateral _____

Note Terms/Interest Rate _____ Due Date _____

_____

_____

TRUSTS

Name of Trust _____

Beneficiaries _____

Trustee(s) _____

Trustee Contact Information _____

_____

Trust Paperwork Location _____

Notes _____

_____

Name of Trust _____

Beneficiaries _____

Trustee(s) _____

Trustee Contact Information _____

_____

Trust Paperwork Location _____

_____

Notes _____

_____

Name of Trust _____

Beneficiaries _____

Trustee(s) _____

Trustee Contact Information _____

_____

Trust Paperwork Location _____

_____

Notes _____

_____

_____

_____

_____

OTHER ASSETS

PRECIOUS STONES/ROCKS/MINERALS (provide description and location)

_____

_____

_____

_____

_____

COLLECTIBLES (provide description and location)

_____

_____

_____

_____

_____

_____

_____

_____

_____

COIN/STAMP COLLECTION (provide description and location)

_____

_____

_____

_____

_____

ARTWORK (provide description and location)

_____

_____

_____

_____

ART WORK

_____

_____

_____

_____

_____

_____

_____

_____

_____

_____

_____

_____

_____

_____

_____

_____

OTHER ASSETS (provide description and location)

_____

_____

_____

_____

_____

_____

_____

_____

_____

_____

_____

_____

_____

_____

_____

_____

_____

PERSONAL LIABILITIES

PERSONAL LIABILITIES

LOANS PAYABLE

Type _____

Face Amount _____   Balance as of __/__/__ _____

Monthly Payment/Due Date _____

Terms _____

Lender _____

Address _____

E-mail _____

Phone # _____

Type _____

Face Amount _____   Balance as of __/__/__ _____

Monthly Payment/Due Date _____

Terms _____

Lender _____

Address _____

E-mail _____

Phone # _____

Type _____

Face Amount _____   Balance as of __/__/__ _____

Monthly Payment/Due Date _____

Terms _____

Lender _____

Address _____

E-mail _____

Phone # _____

Type _____

Face Amount _____   Balance as of __/__/__ _____

Monthly Payment/Due Date _____

Terms _____

Lender _____

Address _____

E-mail _____

Phone # _____

Type _____

Face Amount _____   Balance as of __/__/__ _____

Monthly Payment/Due Date _____

Terms _____

Lender _____

Address _____

E-mail _____

Phone # _____

CREDIT CARDS

Institution/Type	Account #	Balance
_____	_____	_____
_____	_____	_____
_____	_____	_____
_____	_____	_____
_____	_____	_____
_____	_____	_____
_____	_____	_____
_____	_____	_____
_____	_____	_____
_____	_____	_____
_____	_____	_____
_____	_____	_____
_____	_____	_____
_____	_____	_____
_____	_____	_____
_____	_____	_____

RECAP OF MONTHLY/QUARTERLY LIABILITIES

TYPE	AMOUNT
Mortgage/Rent	_____
Homeowner's Association Fee	_____
Utilities: Electric	_____
Utilities: Gas	_____
Utilities: Water	_____
Utilities: Internet Provider	_____
Utilities: Cable Provider	_____
Utilities: Telephone Provider (Land Line)	_____
Utilities: Telephone Provider (Cell)	_____
Landscaping	_____
Pool Service	_____
Federal/State Taxes Payable	_____
Quarterly Estimated Taxes Payable	_____
Private School Fees	_____
Afterschool Activity Fees	_____
Gym Membership Fees	_____
College/Other Institution Fees	_____
Other	_____
Other	_____
Other	_____
Other	_____
Other	_____
Other	_____
Other	_____
Other	_____
Other	_____
Other	_____
Other	_____
Other	_____
Other	_____

DIGITAL
FOOTPRINT

DIGITAL FOOTPRINT

Today, much of your personal and professional life may be conducted online. For security reasons, you might have hundreds of different passwords, which you most likely are changing quite often. If you became incapacitated or pass away, does anyone know all the accounts to which you're connected and would they be able to access the sites to either update, pay bills or cancel? Use this section to list the URLs and passwords of accounts you've established. If you change a password after you've completed this section, be sure to also make the change here and date your edit of original information.

E-MAIL ADDRESSES

ADDRESS	PASSWORD
_____@yahoo.com	_____
_____@gmail.com	_____
_____@hotmail.com	_____
_____@live.com	_____
_____@yourwebsitename	_____
_____@aol.com	_____
_____@netzero.net	_____
_____@comcast.net	_____
_____@roadrunner.com	_____
_____@_____	_____
_____@_____	_____
_____@_____	_____
_____@_____	_____
_____@_____	_____

SOCIAL NETWORKING SITES

NETWORK	USER NAME	PASSWORD
Facebook		
Google +		
LinkedIn		
Pinterest		
Instagram		
Twitter		
YouTube		
Tumblr		
Vine		
Snapchat		
Reddit		
Flickr		
Other		
Other		
Other		
Other		
Other		
Other		

BANKING/ONLINE BROKERAGE ACCOUNTS

NAME	USER NAME	PASSWORD

BANKING/ONLINE BROKERAGE ACCOUNTS *(continued)*

NAME	USER NAME	PASSWORD

PERSONAL/BUSINESS WEBSITE(S)

NAME	USER NAME	PASSWORD

COMPANIES WITH WHOM I HAVE ON LINE ACCOUNTS

NAME	USER NAME	PASSWORD
Paypal		
Shutterfly		
Groupon		
Meetup		
Amazon		
Ebay		
Public Library		
Electric Co		
Gas Co		
Water Co		
Telephone Co		
Cell Phone Co		
Credit Card Co		
Credit Card Co		
Credit Card Co		
Grocery Store		
Grocery Store		
Costco		
Skype		
Event Brite		
Blog		
Other		
Other		
Other		
Other		
Other		
Other		
Other		
Other		
Other		

URLs For My Accounts

NAME	URL
Paypal	_____
Shutterfly	_____
Groupon	_____
Meetup	_____
Amazon	_____
Ebay	_____
Public Library	_____
Electric Co	_____
Gas Co	_____
Water Co	_____
Telephone Co	_____
Cell Phone Co	_____
Credit Card Co	_____
Credit Card Co	_____
Credit Card Co	_____
Grocery Store	_____
Grocery Store	_____
Costco	_____
Skype	_____
Event Brite	_____
Personal Blog	_____
Business Blog	_____
My Website	_____
Banking	_____
Brokerage	_____
Bill Pay	_____
Car Payment	_____
Mortgage	_____
Other	_____
Other	_____

MISCELLANEOUS DIGITAL ACCOUNTS

NAME	USER NAME	PASSWORD

TRACKING FOR ILL FAMILY MEMBERS

TRACKING FOR ILL FAMILY MEMBER

If you are caring for an incapacitated family member (or even a good friend), it will be necessary for you to keep track of his/her personal information, as well as medical history and preferences. Check to see if he/she has a Medical Health Directive and what you need to do to obtain Power of Attorney status.

MEDICAL

PHYSICIANS

Name _____

Specialty _____

Address _____

E-mail _____

Phone # _____

Name _____

Specialty _____

Address _____

E-mail _____

Phone # _____

Name _____

Specialty _____

Address _____

E-mail _____

Phone # _____

PREFERRED HOSPITAL

Hospital _____

Location _____

Phone # _____

Notes _____

MEDICATIONS *(You can also use this type of record for yourself)*

Name (including generic) _____

Pharmacy/Phone #_____

Prescription # _____

Purpose of Medication_____

Dosage _____ Covered by Insurance? _____

Reactions (if applicable)_____

Prescribing Dr/Number _____

Name (including generic) _____

Pharmacy/Phone #_____

Prescription # _____

Purpose of Medication_____

Dosage _____ Covered by Insurance? _____

Reactions (if applicable)_____

Prescribing Dr/Number _____

Name (including generic) _____

Pharmacy/Phone #_____

Prescription # _____

Purpose of Medication_____

Dosage _____ Covered by Insurance? _____

Reactions (if applicable)_____

Prescribing Dr/Number _____

Name (including generic) _____

Pharmacy/Phone #_____

Prescription # _____

Purpose of Medication_____

Dosage _____ Covered by Insurance? _____

Reactions (if applicable)_____

Prescribing Dr/Number _____

MEDICAL APPOINTMENTS

You can make multiple copies of this page to keep with your daily calendar. Keep each year's tracking separately. This method allows you to refer back to prior appointments and recall what was discussed, prognosis, time frames, etc.

Doctor's Name _____

Address _____

Phone #/E-mail _____ _____

Date of Visit/Reason _____

Concerns Answered? _____ Follow-up Needed?/When? _____

Referral To?_____ Phone # _____

Procedures Performed _____

Notes _____

Doctor's Name _____

Address _____

Phone #/E-mail _____ _____

Date of Visit/Reason _____

Concerns Answered? _____ Follow-up Needed?/When? _____

Referral To?_____ Phone # _____

Procedures Performed _____

Notes _____

Doctor's Name _____

Address _____

Phone #/E-mail _____ _____

Date of Visit/Reason _____

Concerns Answered? _____ Follow-up Needed?/When? _____

Referral To?_____ Phone # _____

Procedures Performed _____

Notes _____

_____

_____

ADVANCED DIRECTIVES

Advanced Directives include a **DNR** (Do Not Resuscitate) and a **Living Will**. You can attach copies of both to this page so they are available when needed. Additionally, distribute copies to applicable providers, including a primary physician, hospital, caregivers, other family members, etc.

MEDICAL RECORDS

Either electronically or on paper, in a notebook or a folder, keep track of test results, procedures and any other applicable records. The next time you go to a doctor and fill out new patient forms, ask the receptionist for a copy. Next, take the time to type up the answers to all the questions. Make multiple copies. Each time you go to a doctor's appointment, you can attach your sheet to their questionnaire. This saves you time and the effort of remembering all pertinent information.

If this is your first time taking a family member to the doctor, in preparation, some of the information you will need for these forms includes:

Name
Physical Address
Mailing Address
Social Security #
Medical Insurance (primary and secondary)
List of prior surgeries and date of operation
Allergies/Sensitivities to Medicine
History of Diseases/Ailments
Familial History of Disease
Specific Complaint for Seeing Doctor
List of Medications and Dosages

FUNERAL
INSTRUCTIONS

FUNERAL INSTRUCTIONS

The cost of dying is on the upswing. Burial plots that cost $1000 in the 1990's are now running in the $4000+ range. If a loved one has previously passed without any pre-arrangements, you already know that it's difficult to make casket choices and decide on everything else that goes with a funeral when you're in a highly emotional state. Although it's not a pleasant task, you can lock in current prices, as well as save your family the burden of funeral arrangements, by pre-paying all costs associated with your death, including a memorial stone. If you have completed this process, record all the pertinent information below. If not, at least list your preferences so your family can abide by your last wishes as they prepare to say farewell to you.

Burial or Cremation? _____

Cemetery Location of Burial Plot _____

Lot # of Burial Plot_____

Funeral Home _____

Funeral Home Contact and Phone # _____

_____

Funeral Expenses Prepaid?_____ Balance Still Owing? _____

Type of Ceremony (i.e., religious, military, masonic) _____

_____

Who Shall Preside at Funeral? _____

Who Would You Like To Give The Eulogies? _____

_____

Would You Like People To Make a Contribution To a Charity in Lieu of Flowers? _____ Which Charity? _____

Special Instructions/Requests_____

_____

_____

_____

_____

_____

PERSONAL PROPERTY DISPOSITION

DISPOSITION OF PERSONAL ASSETS

Personal property can be earmarked for those special people upon whom you want to bestow a special remembrance. List below a description of the item and to whom you want it to go. You might notify your family, and especially this person, of your final wishes so that there's no confusion or arguing upon settlement of your estate.

DESCRIPTION OF ITEM   BEQUEATHED TO

VEHICLES

_____   _____

_____   _____

_____   _____

_____   _____

_____   _____

_____   _____

FURNITURE

_____   _____

_____   _____

_____   _____

_____   _____

_____   _____

_____   _____

_____   _____

_____   _____

_____   _____

_____   _____

_____   _____

DESCRIPTION OF ITEM	BEQUEATHED TO

SPECIAL ARTICLES OF CLOTHING

_____	_____
_____	_____
_____	_____
_____	_____
_____	_____
_____	_____

JEWELRY

_____	_____
_____	_____
_____	_____
_____	_____
_____	_____
_____	_____
_____	_____
_____	_____
_____	_____
_____	_____
_____	_____
_____	_____
_____	_____
_____	_____
_____	_____
_____	_____

DESCRIPTION OF ITEM	BEQUEATHED TO

COIN COLLECTION

_____   _____
_____   _____
_____   _____
_____   _____
_____   _____
_____   _____

STAMP COLLECTION

_____   _____
_____   _____
_____   _____
_____   _____
_____   _____
_____   _____

OTHER COLLECTIBLES/MEMORABILIA

_____   _____
_____   _____
_____   _____
_____   _____
_____   _____
_____   _____
_____   _____
_____   _____
_____   _____
_____   _____
_____   _____
_____   _____

DESCRIPTION OF ITEM

BEQUEATHED TO

MISCELLANEOUS

_____   _____

_____   _____

_____   _____

_____   _____

_____   _____

_____   _____

_____   _____

_____   _____

_____   _____

_____   _____

_____   _____

_____   _____

_____   _____

_____   _____

_____   _____

_____   _____

_____   _____

_____   _____

_____   _____

_____   _____

_____   _____

_____   _____

_____   _____

_____   _____

_____   _____

CHARITABLE DONATIONS

CHARITABLE DONATIONS

For those who die with no heirs, their estate can be bequeathed in its entirety to charitable organizations. Some people who have heirs also make final bequests to various charities. List your bequests, naming the organization and amount you wish to leave them. If you want it earmarked for a special fund, note which one.

NAME OF ORGANIZATION   AMOUNT TO BEQUEATH
ADDRESS/CONTACT #

1._____   _____

_____

2._____   _____

_____

3._____   _____

_____

4. _____   _____

_____

5._____   _____

_____

6._____   _____

_____

7._____   _____

_____

NOTES: _____

_____

_____

_____

_____

SPECIAL INSTRUCTIONS

SPECIAL INSTRUCTIONS

In narrative form, you can list any special instructions or requests about the disposal of your estate. You can also cover any additional items/circumstances that are unique to your life, which you may want to record for your heirs.

_____

_____

_____

_____

_____

_____

_____

_____

_____

_____

_____

_____

_____

_____

_____

_____

_____

_____

_____

NOTARIZATION

NOTARY

Fill out the following information and take this book to a Notary Public. Once signed, it is an enforceable legal document (in regard to your bequests).

I, _____, am of sound body and mind and do hereby certify that the bequests made in this booklet are my sole wishes, which I agreed to without coercion of any other party.

_____

_____

Witness

STATE OF _____   )
)
County of _____   )

      SUBSCRIBED, SWORN TO AND ACKNOWLEDGED before me by _____ and SUBSCRIBED AND SWORN TO before me by _____ (witness), this _____ day of _____, _____.

_____

Notary Public

ADDENDUM

ADDENDUM

When you make changes in the recorded information before this section, record them here and date the change. If the change is in regard to any bequests, make sure to get it renotarized.

_____

_____

_____

_____

_____

_____

_____

_____

_____

_____

_____

_____

_____

_____

_____

_____

_____

_____

ABOUT THE AUTHOR

ABOUT THE AUTHOR

Ellen Gerst is a Grief Recovery Specialist®, a Life Coach who specializes in grief and relationships, a workshop leader and an author.

Having navigated the treacherous waters of spousal grief, as well as being a caregiver for her mother who battled Alzheimer's for ten years, Ellen's mission is to help others develop skills so they can ride the stormy seas where she once swam and which she successfully survived the difficulties encountered.

Ellen helps her clients and readers adjust their perspective so that they may learn how to accept their *new normal*. Ellen believes it is just not enough to merely survive, but it is important to help others to learn how to thrive in their new circumstances.

Ellen has penned books on how to cope with grief; how to build and maintain healthy and successful relationships; how to cope with suicide; teen pregnancy prevention; dementia and caregiving for aging parents; spirituality; fitness and weight loss; confidence and the power of positive thought; and social media and networking for entrepreneurs.

You can purchase her books through Amazon or Barnes & Noble at the following links.

Amazon: *http://www.amazon.com/Ellen-Gerst/e/B006IZ0FOW*
B & N: *http://www.barnesandnoble.com/c/ellen-gerst*

Visit Ellen on her website at *http://www.LNGerst.com* for information on her coaching services and other products.

You can also follow her on Pinterest and Facebook for tips and thoughts on coping with grief; love, dating and relationships; and caregiving for an aging parent with Alzheimer's.

www.ingramcontent.com/pod-product-compliance
Lightning Source LLC
Chambersburg PA
CBHW081222280526
45787CB00006B/2482